Candy, the old car

Story by Annette Smith
Illustrations by Chantal Stewart

All the cars were getting ready for the race to Hilltop Park. They came up to the line.

There were two little blue cars,
a big green car,
and a red racing car.

The red racing car
looked at the little blue cars
and the big green car.
"I will win the race," he said.
"I can go very fast."

Ch...   Ch...   Ch...

Candy, the old car,

came slowly up to the line.

"You are too old
to be in a race like this,"
said the red racing car.
"You can't go fast like me."

Candy, the old car, smiled.

"We will see," he said.

"We will see."

Ready!   Go!

Away went the little blue cars
and the big green car.

Ch...   Ch...   Ch...

Candy, the old car,

went slowly down the road.

The red racing car said,

"I can go so fast

that I can stay here

and take a nap first."

"I will **still** win the race,"
he said,
and he shut his eyes.

11

The little blue cars
did not go the right way.
They did not see the arrow.
The big green car was going so fast
that it went off the road!

But Candy went slowly up the hill
to Hilltop Park.

13

The red racing car woke up.
"It's time for me
to start the race now,"
he said, and away he went.

But he was too late.

Candy, the old car,

had won the race.